A Walk on the Waves

Matthew 14:13–32

(Jesus Walks on the Water)

Mary Manz Simon

Illustrated by Dennis Jones

CPH®
SAINT LOUIS

For Brian Peterson
Colossians 3:12–17

Books by Mary Manz Simon from Concordia Publishing House

Hear Me Read Level 1 Series
What Next?
Drip Drop
Jibber Jabber
Hide the Baby
Toot! Toot!
Bing!
Whoops!
Send a Baby
A Silent Night
Follow That Star
Row the Boat
Rumble, Rumble
Who Will Help?
Sit Down
Come to Jesus
Too Tall, Too Small
Hurry, Hurry!
Where Is Jesus?

Hear Me Read Big Books Series
What's Next?
Drip Drop
Send a Baby

Follow That Star
Sit Down
Come to Jesus
Too Tall, Too Small
Where Is Jesus?

Hear Me Read Level 2 Series
The No-Go King
Hurray for the Lord's Army!
The Hide-and-Seek Prince
Daniel and the Tattletales
The First Christmas
Through the Roof
A Walk on the Waves
Thank You, Jesus

Little Visits® Series
Little Visits on the Go
Little Visits for Toddlers
Little Visits with Jesus
Little Visits Every Day

Stop! It's Christmas
God's Children Pray
My First Diary

Copyright © 1993 Concordia Publishing House
3558 S. Jefferson Avenue, St. Louis, MO 63118-3968
Manufactured in the United States of America

Library of Congress Cataloging-in-Publication Data

Simon, Mary Manz, 1948–
    A walk on the waves : Matthew 14:13-32 : Jesus walks on the water / Mary Manz Simon : illustrated by Dennis Jones.
        p.   cm. — (hear me read. Level 2)
Summary: Retells what happened when Jesus walked across a stormy lake to join his disciples in their boat.
    ISBN 0-570-04735-8
    1. Jesus walking on the water (Miracle)—Juvenile literature.
[1. Jesus walking on the water (Miracle) 2. Jesus Christ—Miracles. 3. Bible stories—N.T.] I. Jones, Dennis, ill. II. Title. III. Title: Jesus walks on the water. IV. Series: Simon, Mary Manz, 1948– Hear me read. Level 2. BT367. W34S56   1993
232.9'55—dc20   92-21374

6 7 8 9 10 11 12 13   07 06 05 04 03 02 01 00

The disciples rowed Jesus in a boat.
Jesus wanted to rest.
The boat came to a quiet place.

Thousands of people came to see Jesus.
Some sat by the road.
Some sat on a hill.
Some sat by a lake.
Thousands and thousands of people came to see Jesus.

The people wanted to learn.
Jesus told them, "God loves you."

Some people were sick.
Jesus made them well.

The people were hungry.
Jesus gave them bread and fish.

The people began to get tired.
It was getting late.

"You go ahead," Jesus told His
disciples.
"There are still many people.
I will say good-bye to them.
Get in the boat.
Go to the other side of the lake."

Peter and the other disciples climbed
into a boat.
They started to row across the lake.

"Good-bye," Jesus said to the people. "God loves you."

Thousands and thousands of people
started to go home.
Some people walked down a hill.
Some climbed into boats.
Others walked down the road.

Thousands and thousands of people
started to go home.

Soon it was quiet.
Night was coming.
Jesus was alone.

Jesus walked up a hill.
He wanted to pray.
The sky grew dark.
Jesus prayed.

The disciples rowed the boat to the middle of the lake.
A strong wind blew over the lake.

"Whoo, whoo!" went the wind.
Waves rocked the boat.

The disciples rowed harder.
"Whoo, whoo, whoo!" went the wind.

The waves jumped higher and higher.
The disciples rowed harder and harder.

Jesus saw the disciples.
He saw them row harder
and harder.

Jesus heard the wind blow,
"Whoo, whoo!"
He saw the waves jump higher
and higher.

Jesus walked to His disciples.
He walked to the boat.
Jesus walked on the water!

The disciples rowed harder.
The wind blew, "Whoo, whoo, whoo!"
The waves jumped higher
and higher.

Suddenly the disciples saw Jesus.
They saw Jesus walking to the boat.
They saw Him walking on the waves!
But they did not know who it was.

"A ghost!" they screamed.
"It's a ghost."

"No," said Jesus.
"It is I.
Don't be afraid."

"Jesus? Jesus?" Peter asked.
"If it's really You, let me come
to You.
Let me walk on the water."

"Come, Peter," said Jesus.
"Come to Me over the water, Peter."

Peter got out of the boat.
He started walking on the water.
The disciples watched.

Peter heard the wind blow,
"Whoo, whoo!"
Peter saw the waves jump higher.
Suddenly, Peter was afraid.
He began to sink.

"Jesus, Jesus," said Peter.
"Save me, Jesus!"

Jesus grabbed Peter's hand.
"Oh, Peter," said Jesus.
"You know I will help you."

Jesus and Peter climbed
into the boat.
The wind stopped.
The waves were quiet.

The disciples looked at Jesus.
"Jesus," they said.
"Jesus, You are the Son of God!"

About the Author

Mary Manz Simon holds a doctoral degree in education with a specialty in early childhood education. She has taught at levels from preschool through postgraduate. Dr. Simon also has authored *Stop! It's Christmas; God's Children Pray;* the best-selling *Little Visits with Jesus; Little Visits Every Day; Little Visits for Toddlers; Little Visits on the Go; My First Diary,* and the Hear Me Read Level 1 Bible stories series. She and her husband, the Reverend Henry A. Simon, are the parents of three children.